THE TRY NOT TO LAUGH CHALLENGE™

REPULSIVE RIDDLES

FOR BOYS AND GIRLS

TM & Copyright© 2020 by Try Not To Laugh Challenge®
ALL RIGHTS RESERVED.

Published in the United States. By purchase of this book, you have been licensed one copy for personal use only. No part of this work may be reproduced, redistributed, or used in any form or by any means without prior written permission of the publisher and copyright owner.

Try Not To Laugh Challenge® BONUS PLAY

Join our Joke Club and get the Bonus Play PDF!

Simply send us an email to:

TNTLPublishing@gmail.com

and you will get the following:

- 10 Hilarious Would You Rather Questions
- An entry in our Monthly Giveaway of a $50 Amazon Gift card!

We draw a new winner each month and will contact you via email!

Good luck!

TRY NOT TO LAUGH CHALLENGE®
PRESENTS
REPULSIVE RIDDLES FOR KIDS

rid·dle (noun):
A fun question or statement that is intentionally phrased to require you to determine the answer and/or meaning.

Rules of the Game

Repulsive Riddles for Kids is a series that is made up of 10 Rounds containing 4 riddles per player in each round. It is intended to be played as a two-player game. In each round, both players have a chance to score a total of 4 points!

Beginning with Round 1, Player 1 will start by reading aloud the first riddle to Player 2, then Player 2 will attempt to guess what the answer is. If correct, Player 1 will record a point and if incorrect, no point is recorded for that riddle. Repeat with the second riddle, then Player 1 will pass the book to Player 2 and repeat the process.

TRY NOT TO LAUGH CHALLENGE®

PRESENTS

REPULSIVE RIDDLES FOR KIDS

After each round, add up each player's scores and tally them up on the End of Round score sheet provided. Remember, the riddle points belong to the player answering the riddle.

Continue playing through all 10 Rounds and tally up your final score to determine who will be deemed
THE MOST REPULSIVE RIDDLER!
In the event of a tie, continue to Round 11 for the Tie-Breaker Round where the Winner Takes All!

Players

This fun game is great for anyone age 8 & up! Grab a friend, a family member, or parent and flip a coin or paper, rock, scissors to decide who will be Player 1 and Player 2.

Let the games begin! ⟶

ROUND 1

PLAYER 1

1 If you let me go, you'll probably feel better, but no one ever appreciates me! What am I?

Gas!   Point____ /1

2 Pick a color, pick a flower, pick anything else at all! Though I suppose how you remove your mucus is your call. What is being discouraged?

Nose picking!   Point____ /1

RIDDLER 1 CONTINUE TO NEXT PAGE ➔

PLAYER 1

❸ We are white and strong; any holes might hit a nerve. You must clean use daily if you want us to preserve. What could I be?

Teeth!

Point ___ /1

❹ Half of me is on your foot, far too easy to stub. The rest you'll find in a jar, eaten at a breakfast club. What am I?

Toe jam!

Point ___ /1

PASS THE BOOK TO RIDDLER 2 →

RIDDLER 2

1. I'm the largest arachnid; my hairs irritate skin. I have none at birth, but with every molt new grow in. What am I?

Tarantula.   Point ___/1

2. These are often used to describe the smell of sulfur. After Easter has passed, these are known to occur.
What are they?

Rotting eggs!   Point ___/1

RIDDLER 2 CONTINUE TO NEXT PAGE ➜

RIDDLER 2

3 I may be decomposing as I shamble on. I desire your grey matter, which I shall dine upon. What could I be?

Zombie!

Point ___ /1

4 I am used to make pies that none should ever eat, and a kind of wrestling that involves a slippery feat. What could I be?

Mud.

Point ___ /1

TIME TO SCORE YOUR POINTS! →

PLAYER 1   /4
ROUND TOTAL

PLAYER 2   /4
ROUND TOTAL

ROUND CHAMP

ROUND 2

PLAYER 1

1 What does one take and release all of the time, but if you don't... you'll have a serious problem?

Breath!   Point ____/1

2 I am with you always, sometimes you cover me, and you only tend to notice me if I'm stinky. What could I be?

Your feet!   Point ____/1

RIDDLER 1 CONTINUE TO NEXT PAGE ➔

PLAYER 1

3 When verbalizations are unclear, I may be to blame. You should use a cotton swab if your hearing you are to reclaim.
What am I?

Earwax!

Point____/1

4 What trails behind shell-less garden pests, is a descriptive texture, and stretchy goo children request?

Slime!

Point____/1

PASS THE BOOK TO RIDDLER 2 →

RIDDLER 2

1 A royal flush has no cards when a throne is porcelain. I am the remains of processed food that takes a soggy spin. What am I?

Feces!

Point ___/1

2 If cold, you might put this on. If warm and you wear it, it might make you do what the name implies. What could I be?

A sweater!

Point ___/1

RIDDLER 2 CONTINUE TO NEXT PAGE →

RIDDLER 2

3 I am the term for mail posted with a stamp. I carry my home on my back, leaving trails behind that are damp. What could I be?

Snails! Point ___ /1

4 I'm red and angry, frequently found on post-pubescent's, who may have anxiety at the sight of my mere presence. What am I?

Acne! Point ___ /1

TIME TO SCORE YOUR POINTS! ➔

PLAYER 1

___ /4
ROUND TOTAL

PLAYER 2

___ /4
ROUND TOTAL

ROUND CHAMP

ROUND 3

PLAYER 1

1 I am the moisture where you have direct contact with food. When you're in public, to eject this is rude. What am I?

Saliva

Point ___/1

2 My first is someone sporting who trains physical skills. My second is what gives you a leg to stand on, and is used to walk over hills. What am I?

Athlete's foot!

Point ___/1

RIDDLER 1 CONTINUE TO NEXT PAGE ➜

PLAYER 1

3 Small and vampiric, I irritate the skin on which I live upon. I prey on your pets, but apply collar, bath, or medication, and sadly I'm gone. What am I?

Fleas!

Point ___ /1

4 Without my presence you would be spineless, I'm what remains when you are lifeless. What could I be?

Skeleton!

Point ___ /1

PASS THE BOOK TO RIDDLER 2 →

RIDDLER 2

1 I'm a temptation to scratch and itch, that's naturally occurring. I form after injury, leaving scars that are enduring. What am I?

Scab!

Point____/1

2 You can use me with music, the kitchen, or in the bathroom. You could even see me on a fish. What could I be?

Scales.

Point____/1

RIDDLER 2 CONTINUE TO NEXT PAGE ⟶

RIDDLER 2

3 I am round and green, and I love winter season. I am hung to show the holidays are waiting behind your door. What am I?

Wreath.

Point ___/1

4 I'm the enemy of elementary schools; you will want to use a fine-toothed comb. The simplest way to prevent me is to keep your hat yours alone. What could I be? Lice!

Lice!

Point ___/1

TIME TO SCORE YOUR POINTS! →

PLAYER 1

/4

ROUND TOTAL

PLAYER 2

/4

ROUND TOTAL

ROUND CHAMP

ROUND 4

PLAYER 1

1 I bind the bristles of a brush; after a shower, you find me in the drain. Be diligent when you remove me, for clogs I've caused are a pain. What could I be?

Hair.

Point ___ /1

2 What do you strike to see it's true potential?

A match!

Point ___ /1

RIDDLER 1 CONTINUE TO NEXT PAGE ➡

PLAYER 1

❸ I have no body though was once alive. But if you cut me, you'll be the one to cry. What could I be?

An onion.

Point____/1

❹ What comes out of you, ends up in me, and what comes out of me, ends up in the sea. What could I be?

A toilet.

Point____/1

PASS THE BOOK TO RIDDLER 2 →

RIDDLER 2

1 I've been called a butterfly though I have no wings. I'm the thread that binds injuries that sting. What am I?

Stitches.

Point ___/1

2 When a cat hacks up one of these, it's best to clean it quickly. Otherwise the follicles bind with carpet fibers, and removal becomes quite tricky. What can it be?

Hairball!

Point ___/1

RIDDLER 2 CONTINUE TO NEXT PAGE ➜

RIDDLER 2

❸ *SNAP* this has gone off, made of wood, spring, and metal. Ending rodent life, it is the opposite of gentle. What is it?

A mousetrap!   Point____/1

❹ I hold the moon in darkness. I have little light. I'm not in shining armor, but your dreams I do invite! What am I?

Night!   Point____/1

TIME TO SCORE YOUR POINTS! →

PLAYER 1

/4

___
ROUND TOTAL

PLAYER 2

/4

___
ROUND TOTAL

___
ROUND CHAMP

ROUND 5

PLAYER 1

1 I don't taste like the first part, just the second. I'm eaten a lot near Christmas, I reckon. But also after meals a fair amount of the time. I'm a good little treat that makes your breath smell fine. What could I be?

A peppermint! Point____/1

2 I am a fruit and a verb. What could I be?

Prune! Point____/1

RIDDLER 1 CONTINUE TO NEXT PAGE ➡

PLAYER 1

3 What do Christmas and the moment you're reading this have in common?

The present.   Point____ /1

4 You must shape me with your hand, and I only fly through the air on your command. What am I?

A snowball!   Point____ /1

PASS THE BOOK TO RIDDLER 2 →

RIDDLER 2

1 My sunny side can be seen by a crack.
Upon a bowl, give me a whack!
What am I?

An egg!

Point____/1

2 I have sharp teeth, pointy ears, and I'm flow backward. What am I?

Wolf!

Point____/1

RIDDLER 2 CONTINUE TO NEXT PAGE ➡

RIDDLER 2

3 I'm a holiday song, I sing of receiving luxurious gifts. If you count them all up, it should be 78 unless one I missed! What am I?

Point ___ /1

The 12 Days of Christmas

4 This falls like snow when your scalp is itching, the flakes are loosened by your scritching. What am I?

Point ___ /1

Dander!

TIME TO SCORE YOUR POINTS! ➔

PLAYER 1

/4

_____
ROUND TOTAL

PLAYER 2

/4

_____
ROUND TOTAL

_____
ROUND CHAMP

ROUND 6

PLAYER 1

1 What is something that is left exposed, and a thing you have called your toes?

Bare! Point____/1

2 A measurement when you're more than one, and things you need if you are to run. What am I?

Feet! Point____/1

RIDDLER 1 CONTINUE TO NEXT PAGE →

PLAYER 1

3 Some are helpful in a lab, detecting bombs, or make fine pets; with bare tails, they have transmitted pathogens that would infect. What are they?

Rats!

Point____/1

4 Sometimes I smell, sometimes I stink. I don't need a shower, but I have a sink. What am I?

Kitchen!

Point____/1

PASS THE BOOK TO RIDDLER 2 →

RIDDLER 2

1 In your home, I cause health problems as I grow where it's damp. When you break me, you're an original, a true champ. What am I?

Mold!

Point____/1

2 What can bite in extreme circumstances, yet has no teeth?

Frost!

Point____/1

RIDDLER 2 CONTINUE TO NEXT PAGE ➜

RIDDLER 2

3 Underarms, backs, and foreheads are places I show exertion. I moisten your clothes. I'm personal perspiration. What could I be?

Sweat!

Point _____ /1

4 I'm bundled cotton attached to both ends of a small rod, stick, or tube. When used to clear auditory canals, I absorb the wax that you exude. What am I?

Cotton swab!

Point _____ /1

TIME TO SCORE YOUR POINTS! ➔

PLAYER 1

/4

ROUND TOTAL

PLAYER 2

/4

ROUND TOTAL

ROUND CHAMP

ROUND 7

PLAYER 1

1 Hang me with care if you were good this year; otherwise, coal will greet you, and your eyes will tear. What am I?

Stocking!

Point ___/1

2 What hunter is mighty but small, goes their own way, but for dinner will answer your call?

A cat!

Point ___/1

RIDDLER 1 CONTINUE TO NEXT PAGE ⟶

PLAYER 1

3 What starts out blue and purple, then turns yellow before it disappears?

Bruises! (upside down)

Point ___/1

4 If you have a hard shell, I will break down your walls. For a stubborn pistachio, I'm the right guy to call. What am I?

Nutcracker! (upside down)

Point ___/1

PASS THE BOOK TO RIDDLER 2 →

RIDDLER 2

❶ Chewing, stretching, chomping, and blowing bubbles: foil me again when you're done, or I'll make sticky trouble.
What am I?

Used gum!

Point____/1

❷ If you've been inverted, when righted, you may have felt this. When you're on the sea and your stomach rebels, you'll find it's solid land you miss.
What are you feeling?

Nausea!

Point____/1

RIDDLER 2 CONTINUE TO NEXT PAGE ⟶

RIDDLER 2

3 Bladders, livers, and hearts are different kinds of these; an instrument found in churches for playing soulful melodies. What are they?

Organs!　　　　　Point ___/1

4 Doze in class, and you may leave a trail. Upon noticing the moisture, your face will quickly pale. What is it?

Drool!　　　　　Point ___/1

TIME TO SCORE YOUR POINTS! ⟶

PLAYER 1

___/4
ROUND TOTAL

PLAYER 2

___/4
ROUND TOTAL

___
ROUND CHAMP

ROUND 8

PLAYER 1

1 I should be taken out weekly, but not to dinner. A plastic sack encapsulates these remains, so long as it doesn't leak, it's a winner. What am I?

Garbage!   Point____/1

2 I am heat-sealed packaging that holds medication. I also occur with ill-fitting shoes through frictions application. What am I?

Blisters!   Point____/1

RIDDLER 1 CONTINUE TO NEXT PAGE ⟶

PLAYER 1

❸ I live in your cranium, providing lots of thoughts. I'm a kind of coral where fish hide, so as not to be caught. What am I?

Brains! Point____/1

❹ I am famous for making everyone scream, but usually in a good way... unless you're lactose intolerant. What am I?

Ice Cream! Point____/1

PASS THE BOOK TO RIDDLER 2 →

RIDDLER 2

❶ This is slang for feces that likes to hang around. A car door's small damage impression plus a white sea bird, followed by what pirates do to treasure they have found. What is it?

Dingleberry!

Point____ /1

❷ I am a piece of timber lodged within your skin. You'd best remove it quickly to avoid infection. What am I?

Splinter!

Point____ /1

RIDDLER 2 CONTINUE TO NEXT PAGE ⟶

RIDDLER 2

3 Infrequent defecation could mean you are this, adding exercise, or fiber to your diet would not be remiss. What am I?

Constipation!

Point____/1

4 This is left by an oily hand, a smudge left on a glass. Each one is unique and identifies a lad or lass. What is it?

Fingerprint.

Point____/1

TIME TO SCORE YOUR POINTS! →

PLAYER 1   /4
ROUND TOTAL

PLAYER 2   /4
ROUND TOTAL

ROUND CHAMP

ROUND 9

PLAYER 1

1 I'm awake while you are asleep, searching for critters below who creep. Quietly, I ask my question 'who' won't cause me indigestion. What could I be?

An owl! Point ___/1

2 I am a single piece of paper, and have music on me. I am something that one folds; when I'm dirty, you should wash me. What am I?

Sheets. Point ___/1

RIDDLER 1 CONTINUE TO NEXT PAGE →

PLAYER 1

3 I'll double my size when you make a bubble, but getting in your hair can cause quite the trouble. What am I?

Gum. (upside down)

Point ___ /1

4 I can change in height, with or without feet, as I fall to the bottom. Expect me in winter, I might visit in autumn. What am I?

Snow! (upside down)

Point ___ /1

PASS THE BOOK TO RIDDLER 2 →

RIDDLER 2

1 These orbs are connected to you and held dear. Brown, green, blue, hazel, I allow you to peer. What am I?

Your eyeballs!

Point____/1

2 Before tadpoles, but after frogs in the cycle, these occur: slimy, soft, and black dotted ones have vitals. What are they?

Frogspawn!

Point____/1

RIDDLER 2 CONTINUE TO NEXT PAGE →

RIDDLER 2

3 If you need to talk about your feeling this word is what you do. If something needs to let of pressure they do this too. What is it?

Vent. (upside down)

Point____ /1

4 The sound of a pigeon added to what it is called when competitors finish equally: this is a game between genders played when wee. What is it?

Cooties! (upside down)

Point____ /1

TIME TO SCORE YOUR POINTS! →

PLAYER 1

/4

ROUND TOTAL

PLAYER 2

/4

ROUND TOTAL

ROUND CHAMP

ROUND 10

PLAYER 1

1) I'm the contents of an upset stomach when it's been expelled. Others have been known to follow suit at the inhalation of my smell. What could I be?

Point____/1

Vomit!

2) Though I sound like a million, one thousand is my name. I'm a nightmare for a podiatris though you might think the same. What am I?

Millipede!

Point____/1

RIDDLER 1 CONTINUE TO NEXT PAGE ➜

PLAYER 1

❸ A fur this, a this of paint. You wear me when the cold is your main complaint. What am I?

Point____/1

A coat.

❹ I'm accumulated gas that needs a hearty release, for my competitions cite the alphabet till adults have you cease. What am I?

Burps!

Point____/1

PASS THE BOOK TO RIDDLER 2 ➙

RIDDLER 2

1 In olden time, relief for your bowels was not found in a building. If you're unlucky, I'm just a seat with a hole below awaiting filling. What am I?

An outhouse!

Point____ /1

2 It may be best not to share your salsa even with a friend, for some use the same chip, not even bothering to switch to the clean end! What is being described?

Double-dipping!

Point____ /1

RIDDLER 2 CONTINUE TO NEXT PAGE →

RIDDLER 2

3 This place is underground where sewage goes and shares the spelling of a person who sews. What is it?

Sewer!

Point ___ /1

4 Have you heard of a creature that polishes stools? This insect makes and rolls them into balls without any tools. What is it?

Dung beetle!

Point ___ /1

TIME TO SCORE YOUR POINTS! →

PLAYER 1

___/4
ROUND TOTAL

PLAYER 2

___/4
ROUND TOTAL

___
ROUND CHAMP

Add up each player's scores from all previous rounds. The player with the most points is crowned

THE ULTIMATE REPULSIVE RIDDLER!

If points result in a tie, move on to the Tie-Breaker Round.

PLAYER 1   GRAND TOTAL

PLAYER 2   GRAND TOTAL

_____

THE ULTIMATE REPULSIVE RIDDLER

ROUND 11

TIE-BREAKER
(WINNER TAKES ALL!)

PLAYER 1

1 I hold the moon in darkness. I have little light. I'm not in shining armor, but your dreams I do invite! What am I?

Night.   Point____/1

2 I'm a boogie, but not the dance. I would be in used tissues, if you had a clean one in advance. What am I?

Snot.   Point____/1

RIDDLER 1 CONTINUE TO NEXT PAGE ➡

PLAYER 1

3 If you're fond of felines, with this you are acquainted. When containing fecal matter, the clay has become tainted. What is it?

Litter box.

Point____/1

4 Heat made me sponge though I was first liquid. I am stacked in layers, and to my icing, you're addicted. What am I?

Cake!

Point____/1

PASS THE BOOK TO RIDDLER 2 ⟶

RIDDLER 2

1 Are you feeling unwell, hot, and sweating through your sheets? You should see a doctor if you can't stand this heat. What is it?

Point____/1

A fever.

2 I am a mammal whose small weight is bared on webbed fingers. A person who wouldn't do this to an eye has a face where no expression lingers. What am I?

Point____/1

A bat!

RIDDLER 2 CONTINUE TO NEXT PAGE ➝

RIDDLER 2

3 Can you name blood that rises but does not breach? What's the term for damage on a peach?

Bruises! Point ___ /1

4 You don't have to make my bed for I do not have sheets. While some dump, others fight flames; if wheels are moving you should be buckled in a seats. What is it?

Trucks! Point ___ /1

TIME TO SCORE YOUR POINTS! ➔

Add up each player's score from the previous round.
The player with the most points is crowned

THE ULTIMATE REPULSIVE RIDDLER!

PLAYER 1 /4
ROUND TOTAL

PLAYER 2 /4
ROUND TOTAL

THE ULTIMATE REPULSIVE RIDDLER

CHECK OUT OUR

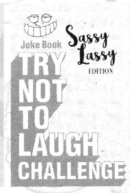

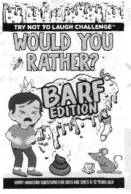

VISIT OUR AMAZON STORE AT:
WWW.AMAZON.COM/AUTHOR/CRAZYCOREY

OTHER JOKE BOOKS!

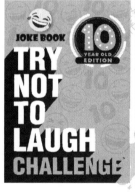
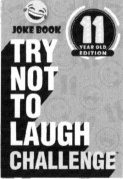
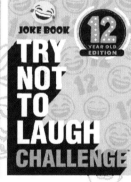

IF YOU HAVE ENJOYED OUR BOOK, WE WOULD LOVE FOR YOU TO REVIEW US ON AMAZON!

Made in the USA
Monee, IL
23 December 2020